High Poets Society

B. Abbott

MONARCH PUBLISHING

High Poets Society

Semicolons and Ampersands

The moon's so fickle

with her love; always

disappearing

once the sun

comes

up.

Love is;

finding a soul

more comfortable

than your own.

Love

is

every shade

ever made

and

never ever

seems to fade.

Sink your teeth

into my lip

and

let me feel

why I'm alive.

Reincarnation

has to exist; it can be

the only reason

I'm familiar

with your kiss.

You had

that sorta fire;

which made mine

burn brighter.

I

lust over

your

sunkissed skin

and

love all the places

the rays never been.

I

want to

share with you;

my present and my past,

everything that happens or ever has.

When you meet someone, you already know;

You feel familiarity within your soul.

For over the years,

You've shared joy and tears

And that feeling continues to grow.

I'll never understand,

no matter how hard I try.

How the word love

doesn't contain the letters... U or I.

You declared war and the battleground was my heart.

And with every shot you took, the arrows hit their mark.

And I thought that I would die but little did I know

it was the start to a love so great it conquered all the hurt.

I thought your laugh was my favorite thing about you

until I made you moan and

once I heard those gasps and sighs

you turned on my soul.

If everyone experienced the earthquakes I feel,

which are caused by the mere sight of you;

the world would tremble and violently shake

till the mountains fell down

and the oceans were drained.

I'd pick your thunder,

I'd pick your rain; over anyone's sunshine

any day.

Every person you meet, is either a roadblock or a bridge;

stopping you from where you're going

or getting you safely over the edge.

I've always been a fighter;

for love,

for reputation,

for the weak,

for what I feel should be,

for what I feel shouldn't.

I don't seek quarrels but I stand tall when they come.

As a mountain, as a tree, as a ten-foot wall between myself and defeat.

Till the only one standing is ME.

Let your love be like a vine; even if it blooms in the shadows,

it will grow towards the shine.

Funny thing about the darkness; it's defeated

by the simplest shimmer of light.

Forgive

during the chaos

and love during the calm.

Why can't we just love all the time?

We let all the bullshit cloud our minds.

Like storms moving in that steal the shine;

ruining what we thought was sublime.

That midnight smile

and your 2am eyes,

will be the death of me; my demise.

I pray karma isn't real;

for I'd never want you to feel

how I feel.

You awake every morning

with a new dream in mind,

as if yesterday didn't matter

and tomorrow will be fine.

I sing through hurricanes.

Happy songs in the rain.

Because storms can't ruin my parade; I dance in puddles,

I'll never change.

Honey

Berry

Ashes

I can no longer go on like this.

So, I rest the blade against my wrist.

I close my eyes and before I slit;

I dream of a love which no longer exists.

Romeo plays Russian Roulette

yet he'd rather die slow

from cigarettes or memories of Juliet

and a love lost he can't quite forget.

Your complacency

left a vacancy,

right where my heart should be.

I wonder if my brokenness is noticeable.

If they can see the remnants

of the tears which I cry when alone.

Or am I able to fool strangers so

easily, just by smiling back?

Showing a couple teeth

so they don't notice the true me.

That I'm lost in defeat

and underneath

I can't breathe.

I feel the tremors rumble inside my chest.
The vibrations throw my wholeness out of synch
and I don't know if I'll ever catch my breath again.

The worst feeling in the world is hurting and not knowing why.
Being consumed by sadness in the blink of an eye
and overcome with a sense of hopelessness,
which buries every single intuition of being ok again,
way the fuck down.

But somehow, I manage to swim back to the surface
and emerge from that sunken ship of anxiety.
I haven't drowned yet, sometimes it just takes me a minute to
resurface and catch my breath.

I pretend pretty well,

for all strangers to see.

But fall apart and crumble

in front of those closest to me.

Tangled

in a web of lies,

set to catch,

a different fly.

I know these feelings you felt between us scared you.
And I know it's because you felt them before. Those feelings taken
away from you so abruptly, leaving you with feelings you can't ignore.

And I can see why you were so hesitant at first, you never wanted to
go back to that place, again. You know the path we were on could lead
you straight there, our beginning reminds you of that end. So you ran
away, far from this place because of one small mistake, that I could
make, while here I remain, broken the same as you, before you knew
my name.

You told me not to write anything sad but those tear-filled lines were
all I had and this fake smile is just going to have to do.
And I don't exactly remember when, I found happiness
again but I think it was because of you.

But as I sit here in my old rocking chair I remember the times we
used to smile. I then looked close and thought I saw a ghost but it's
just that happiness that's been gone awhile.

I cut

you off

just like that,

every time, until

you call back.

Love called.

I let it ring.

I was

on the other line,

with a different fling.

How can we end, if we didn't start?

As if we weren't in love

but you somehow broke my heart.

I lost something,

I never had.

Yet it hurts, just as bad.

Break

my heart,

take your piece.

There's plenty more for someone else to love me.

I love too much

and

not loved enough.

But I'll never change.

You

don't have

to be loved to be love.

I drown

in your saltwater soul.

Gasping for air

but my breath you have stole.

As if we were grapes,

on a vine;

yet you turned to raisins

and I, to wine.

If I could go back,

knowing how it ends,

I'm still sure, I'd love you again.

One day: it won't hurt as bad.

Then they'll come back and you'll remember

it had.

Our eyes crossed paths for the first time in awhile, today.
And I couldn't help but smile. I saw the pain in your eyes from how
you treated me and that remorse brought me joy.

Your admission without words was more apparent than any sincere
apology could deliver. And in that moment,
I felt as if I had won, when in reality,

I had lost everything I had ever loved.

You know something, it's not you who keeps me awake at night, it's
the thoughts of all the things I did, for you, which never ended
up working out. The sacrifices, the heartache, the bending over
backwards just to prove your love was worth me stretching for it.
None of it was good enough. So how am I to dream again? When I
gave my best and we still came to an end...

There are hundreds if not thousands of "soul mates" in the world for every single one of us. Just think about it...What are the odds you'll meet your one true and only soul mate, when there are 7 billion people in this world?... What are the odds you'll go to the same college, same bar, same online dating website as them? It's in the billions if not trillions. We as humans romanticize love to an unreal idealistic level but even so, once it is presented right in front of our faces we jump at the chance and run with it as if we'll lose it and never find it again and that is what makes us so beautiful, so broken and so real.

It was crazy how you made me feel in such a short amount of time.
It was as if we knew every single thing about each other, souls
connected through the interwoven fantasy we call time. Past lovers?
Maybe. Soul mates, which will always be attracted to one another?

Absolutely.

And I can't wait to meet you over and again. Until next time.

American Idiom

A fragile smile with a backbone of steel.

Don't let her insecurities fool you;

she's tough as nails.

This girl right here is a risk taker,

she colors outside the lines,

she's a heart breaker.

Every single week she needs a different flavor

instead of one single taste

to stay and savor.

I've completely fallen

head over heels.

And as I fall

I wonder if she'll?

Two minds are better than one?

Well, I think two hearts are better in love.

You are armed

to the teeth; with a plan

of conquering me. You won't settle

with defeat, so war it must be.

I'll give you a piece

of my mind

but my heart and soul may take

a little time.

I'm having mixed feelings.

I can't stop the spinning of the ceiling.

I'm so dizzy drunk

About to throw up.

I run to the restroom,

there's nothing else I can do.

All because of the words "I love you"

uttered by the person

who I love too.

I'd burn in hell.

I'd rot in jail.

For a forbidden love

I just had to steal.

Love's a game

of cat and mouse,

where you never want

to be caught in the doghouse.

There's a method to my madness,

yet I can't quite say

...but it definitely involves your heart

in some type of way.

Your love

was fuel to my fire.

As a gas can

dousing

a burning lighter.

Make yourself at

home; fill

the vacancy

I call my soul.

I had that eat your heart out feeling,
as I walked through the door,
you on my arm,
not a care in the world.

Every single pair of eyes turned to us but all we could see was each
other. We were in as much awe at our love as the rest of the room and
we were not afraid to live in that moment.

We savored in the adoration
or jealousy, if I'm mistaken.

As if our love

was made from scratch;

with the same old recipe

but for a brand new batch.

The heart

always wants

what it can't have,

yet somehow you are mine.

I just want

you to be

a chapter in my life.

It's not even important

how much you write.

Worst will come to worst

if our love happens to die first.

Flat broke,

can't even buy some love.

But that's ok, there's plenty of

cheaper drugs.

And then you added insult to the injury;

as if breaking my heart wasn't a big enough victory,

you just had to say you never loved me.

To be

homesick

yet not for a place,

but more of that feeling

from seeing their face.

She saved her love

for a rainy day

but it died of thirst,

somewhere along the way.

Your love,

was fool's gold.

And I, should've known.

What once was here,

now'as disappeared.

As if love can vanish into

thin air.

I hold my breath

and wait for you.

But always gasp for air

and turn a shade of blue.

What a sight,

to watch you go up in flames.

While I drown in water;

we both end the same.

Worry about

who you'll grow to be.

Your shits aren't affected by what I eat.

I hate your guts

but I still

fell

in

love.

I received a clean bill of health.

Because with only a broken heart,

the Docs can't tell.

Absence makes the heart grow fonder.

Please.

As if acid grows flowers

better than water.

I still have a soft spot

for all of my loves

I have not forgot.

She

As if she was a diamond

and didn't know.

I saw her shinin', even when all

she saw was coal.

Stardust stained her dress.

Yet dancing in the galaxy

was worth the mess.

I know she's crazy;

But she's beautiful

What did I get myself into?

She had a way with words

that made you feel as warm

as the hot baths she indulged in

but don't mistake her kindness for weakness

she roared with the thunder of a lion.

She smells

like summer and

you can feel her shine.

She smiled simply,

in the sun; making it hard

to tell where the glow was coming from.

She

was a lovely

tornado of chaos

and rainbows.

She's a dove

and I'm a raven

yet still we engage

in beautiful conversation.

Whatever she wore,

she wore it best.

From madness,

to that little black dress.

Even when her eyebrows

were a mess; there was still

no contest, between her

and the rest.

She was the type of girl

they name hurricanes after;

a natural disaster.

She

had very little to lose

and she was fierce as fuck, too.

Small yet mighty;

her stature, her voice,

the way in which she loved.

Being in her presence was

comforting and intimidating

all in the same instance.

Always making you ask yourself

"who is this?"

Never Seen the Light

This is to the differents,

the moon children and the freaks,

the ones who never listen,

the nerds and the geeks,

the people people look past,

the never noticed and the weak,

the ones who feel included right now as they read.

Stand up and change the world or die in defeat.

For all it takes is one of us to someday taste victory.

There's squares all around me, everywhere I see.

And I'm just a circle, trying to break free,

From the art on the wall, my phone and t.v.

Let's escape to where the triangles are, rolling amongst the trees.

As if love can grow in the dark;

there's no rays in your chest

yet it blooms in your heart.

I see the trial and error within your eyes.

You've made so many mistakes,

you can't help but be wise.

If kindness cost a penny,

how rich would you be?

And would it make you change your ways

from the time when it was free?

Love like the sun,

share your rays with the world

and let your warmth blanket the entire earth

with a light that shines so bright it can't be ignored.

I feel your love in tremors.

But I want to feel quakes.

You took my hand and said we're going home.

It was pitch black but you lit the road.

I was so unsure yet not my soul.

So, I grabbed on tight and gave up control.

I'm a wolf and you're the moon.

But you only hear me,

out of all those howling at you.

Lucifer called, I said, "Hello"

and he asked me if

I wanted to sell my soul.

I said,

"No thanks, it's not

entirely mine to trade.

It's only half of a whole

with my soul mate."

A needle in my arm,

a powder up my nose,

a drug I can't shake;

you're an addiction I can't control.

You ever say to someone "I couldn't stop talking to you, even if I tried."
And then all of a sudden all you want is to never see them again?
Funny how things change. So quickly it slips right alongside normalcy
and you just remain.

Moving with the tick of the clock. One second at a time, no faster, no
slower. Living in moments where you wish you had control over those
ticks and those tocks.

Those precious seconds. Wishing you could speed them up or slow
them down to a grinding halt. When you want everything to change
immediately or you want to live in a moment forever, wanting to live
in those "stare of your eyes" type forever moments.

But we can't. We can only count those seconds and somehow by
counting those precious seconds, by keeping track, no faster, no
slower than the tick of the clock, we feel as though we finished
slightly ahead of all those things that have changed
but really never meant a thing.

I rather lithium

and feeling numb

than staring down

my father's gun.

They say I'm good

but not good enough

as if somehow I'm liked but never loved.

There's something about

the beauty of a wildflower,

which makes you want to let it bloom.

I held it in this whole time. It's not like me to want to cry. But then, then I saw your face and it all gushed out.

Tear after tear running down my face as if I've been caught in a Tropical Storm of emotions. The flooding, the howls of the wind, the thunder, oh the thunder, it was more than I could contain in my shelter of toughness.

A perfect storm, one a long time overdue and when it subdued, when it passed by on its course of wreckage, I was safe in the healing calm. Under rainbows of moving on.

You can never really recover, you just become something new.
And that's ok. Everything changes, you change, time passes and you
always will worry about too late.

But don't let it stop you from waking up each morning.
Let it be the reason why.
Don't wait for too late.
It comes faster that way.

Love is coming. Just around the corner.
One more tomorrow away.
One more friendly face.
Or first kiss.

You'll give in and you won't even notice.
But that's how it's supposed to happen.
If it's forced, it's no good and bound so loose
it will inevitably come undone.
So don't try, go on with your life
and know you will be loved.

High Poets

Your tie dyed mind

understood

the colors of mine.

Maybe you were sent to me

from centuries of memories.

Attraction isn't always physical;

sometimes you cause butterflies

in my mind.

It's 11:43 and you're on my mind.

But that's the norm, no matter the time.

An absolute certainty;

I'll love you

for eternity.

Chaotic

as it seems,

we were meant to be.

The one,

who is on my mind.

Not every second yet all the time.

If forever

meant a minute

spent

with you,

I'd spend every second,

wishing

for two.

Love

is

chaotic

but so are we.

I just want

to kiss your neck

and tease your thighs.

Run my fingers over

your soul and call it

mine.

I

never

craved attention,

until I tasted yours.

You're the fizz in my cola,

the tsss when I pour.

I don't know if it's the caffeine or the sugar.

But I keep wanting more.

I never loved

soul food until

I had a taste of you.

My heart gets jealous

of my hand

for touching you

in ways it never can.

We lay in bed

so intertwined,

I can't figure out

which limbs are mine.

My darkest days

are brightened

by your light.

I like to get high

but you keep

me grounded.

You're a syringe

full of sin

But I plunge

you right in.

I relate the most with the twisted and broke.

I'm on a crazy train with Kurt Cobain, a shotgun and Hemingway.

Will all of us end the same?

With nothing but the madness we have, to blame.

Baby, have you met your Maker?

Whatever God means to you,

whoever It is?

Have you made peace with your soul?

Have those ashes turned to flames?

Or do you drown them out with pink champagne?

Can you swim?

Even when you're so far under the beautiful surface

and it seems so far away;

you're a fighter.

You flap your arms and kick your legs,

just so you can breathe again.

And how good does that new breath feel?

I bet it's the first breath you've ever taken that was real...

What if heaven was a black hole,

out in our galaxy but we didn't know?

With a gravity we can't control;

pulling in each one of our eternal souls...

Even though we could never be,

I still love that you loved me.

I want

a second chance

at falling in love

with you for the first time.

Love & Reign

R.I.P. to the rainstorm in me.

Now the sun shines,

so brilliantly.

There's a difference between

giving up and moving on.

The first is because you don't love anymore,

the second is because you're strong.

I've had a hundred first days

of sobriety in my addiction to you.

There's something inside of me that seems

to always keep me from day two.

People hurt me.

They drag me through the mud

and break my bones,

they break my heart

and leave the pieces tossed

to the side of the road.

But still I love.

People lie, they cheat their way to the top, pushing

their way past me with no remorse. But still I love. I can't help how I

feel and even when I hate, I still love. I forgive and I love and I hope

that will be enough to make up for everything they've done.

And if not, still I love.

I miss those damn eyes and the way they'd always smile.

That soul piercing stare, which no other can compare.

The way they looked right through me, as if they always knew me.

And I can't wait to see'em again,

for I know it's not the end.

As your world crumbles around you, I am your constant.
Use me. Take my love and feel every ounce of it.

When you don't think that anybody cares, seek me.
I am the rock the currents have yet to wash away.

Standing before you, as you seek refuge,
I become your savior,
a place to always rest while caught amongst a storm.

Cry.

Let those tears water the seeds of recovery.

And with some time, some love, some care, they will bloom.

And there will be a new you.

It was keeping you away, at a safe distance.
You built up a wall, so no one could scale it.
But I found a way; the shovel of determination
tossed away the dirt, as I dug my way
under your insecurities
and barriers of brokenheartedness.

Your walls started to crumble; their weight was too much
once I burrowed my way underneath the foundation
of your guarded soul, destroying the concrete
poured by past affairs.

Leaving you and I standing side-by-side
with no more walls to hide, behind.

I know I'm hard to love but you know I'm worth it. My changes in mood gust by as fast as a nighttime breeze but you bundle up and weather the storm, every time. Every single time.

It's as if you forecast my rage, my pain or disdain.
You know when I'll rain but too, know my sunshine remains.

You looked at me as if all the pain in my eyes, which I felt in the
depths of my soul, which pierced me with every beat of my heart
could be, somehow, someway, dissolved.

And that made me believe. That look.
That look was revealing, healing;
as if you knew everything I was feeling.

What is the universe doing? The tides turning so fast; as if the moon is in control now and you're mine again to have. I've never seen such beauty, as natural as it comes.

I'll remember it forever, every time I see the Sun. Stars seem brighter, now that you're back in my life and as the world spins around them, this dizziness feels so right.

I wonder what you smell like

or even how you taste,

but even more I wonder,

if I could put a smile on your face.

Two things afloat

always seem to drift apart.

But somehow, someway, your current

pulls in my heart.

Your mind, soul and heart

don't all have to agree;

majority rules in love,

so you only need two out of the three.

Somewhere

between

the sea and the sky;

exist two souls

with one heart

and

one mind.

Give me passion which never tires, love which never strays.
Kiss me with some violence, which leaves bruises the next day.
Show me what I've been missing, in a way which I can't forget
and I'll return it all.

So, why haven't you made a move yet?

What I love about you;

society demands of you to change

but you throw up the middle finger

and go on your merry way.

I'm in love with how

you smell, you taste.

I'm in love with

your love, your hate.

Whatever you have

to give, I'll take.

And I wouldn't want it,

any other way.

My first thought,

my last thought,

every thought in between.

I think of you

when I'm awake

and especially when I dream.

You're the master

and I'm the slave.

Only you have the keys

to these chains.

No matter the times

my heart orbits the sun.

For you, it will never fall out of love.

I sit alone,

on my throne of don't care.

With my crown of no fucks,

I'll pass to my heir.

Monetarily poor,

spiritually rich.

I don't know if I would,

if I could make them switch.

What's so wrong with

being strange?

Weirdness flows right

through my veins.

We don't buy the clothes they sell

because we wear the weirdness well.

If success were measured

in love,

would the 1% really be that far above?

Even if I stand alone

for something that I love.

Know I could never take it sitting down,

so I had to stand up.

Allow the sun

to hit your back

as you face the shadow,

which you hide.

Then turn around

so it can kiss your ass

and enjoy the beautiful sunshine.

I created High Poets Society in December 2014 as an outlet, a way to give my words to the world after hiding them for so long. I wrote my first poem in 2005 after reading a book of poetry by Tupac Shakur. The way Tupac expressed love, heartache, victory, defeat; inspired me to express those same parts of myself. It was as if that expression gave me permission to feel and to create. High Poets Society is my canvas, my own love and heartache displayed in the most beautiful way I know. Thank you for reading and all of the support. I couldn't do this without you, much love!

B. Abbott

INSTAGRAM
@highpoetssociety

FACEBOOK
HighPoetsSociety

WEBSITE
highpoetssociety.com

A SILVER TONGUE WITH IRON LUNGS

CPSIA information can be obtained
at www.ICGtesting.com
Printed in the USA
FSOW03n1740270916
25460FS